PUBLIC ENEMY

Exclusive distributors:
Music Sales Limited
8/9 Frith Street, London
W1V 5TZ England.

Music Sales Pty Limited
120 Rothschild Avenue, Rosebery,
NSW 2018, Australia.

This book © Copyright 1989 by
Wise Publications
UK ISBN 0.7119.2095.8
Order No. AM77769

Book design by Helen Senior
Typeset by Capital Setters

Photographs courtesy of:
London Features International
Pictorial Press
Retna Limited
Chris Clunn
CBS/Def Jam Records

Music Sales' complete catalogue lists thousands of titles and is free from your local music shop, or direct from Music Sales Limited. Please send £1 in stamps for postage to Music Sales Limited, 8/9 Frith Street, London W1V 5TZ.

Unauthorised reproduction of any part of this publication by any means including photocopying is an infringement of copyright. Printed in the United Kingdom by Commercial Colour Press, Forest Gate, London E7.

WISE PUBLICATIONS
LONDON/NEW YORK/SYDNEY

CONTENTS

- **4** INTRO
- **8** SOPHISTICATED BITCH
- **10** MIUZI WEIGHS A TON
- **12** TIMEBOMB
- **14** BUM RUSH THE SHOW
- **16** MEGA-BLAST
- **17** TOO MUCH POSSE
- **18** PUBLIC ENEMY #1
- **20** RIGHT STARTER
- **22** M.P.E
- **24** RAISE THE ROOF

- 28 BRING THE NOISE
- 30 DON'T BELIEVE THE HYPE
- 32 FLAVOR FLAV COLD LAMPIN'
- 34 TERMINATOR X TO THE EDGE OF PANIC
- 35 SHE WATCH CHANNEL ZERO ?!
- 36 LOUDER THAN A BOMB
- 38 CAUGHT, CAN I GET A WITNESS
- 40 NIGHT OF THE LIVING BASSHEADS
- 42 BLACK STEEL IN THE HOUR OF CHAOS
- 44 REBEL WITHOUT A PAUSE
- 46 PROPHETS OF RAGE
- 48 PARTY FOR YOUR RIGHT TO FIGHT

INTRO

The first time the long, even, powerful strains of 'Public Enemy Number One' emanated from the inadequate speakers of a West End nightclub, homeboys and fly gals extricated themselves from the popular b-boy stance and all heads nodded.

At a time when hip-hop was wedged between the witty ruminations of Run DMC and the innovative style of Eric B and Rakim, Def Jam had given birth to yet another time-bomb. Following in the wake of LL Cool Jay's 'Rock the Bells' and the Original Concept's 'Pump That Bass', Public Enemy had initiated yet another rap style which was far removed from the 'young ladies and Mercedes' of their predecessors.

Brutally angry and inspiringly original, both lyrical and musical content captured the attention and respect of nightclubbers nationwide. In much the same way as the '89 hype for tough-nut rappers NWA (Naughty Word Advocates, aka Niggers With Attitude), the Public Enemy image preceded their attack on British hip-hop audiences.

Their lyrics were violent in delivery and concentrated largely on the negative side of popularist issues: "Radio. The suckers never play me..." ('Rebel Without A Pause').

Not that the complexities of American street politics were a selling point to the South London bedroom scratcher who hopped down to his local hip record shop to buy the track. It was the party essence craftily interwoven amongst the preaching which appealed to the British rap market.

Meanwhile, the British media eagerly awaited the opportunity to strike the first blow at the Public Enemy image. Public Enemy knew that they would win on both counts: "We're gonna bum rush the show and there's no way of stopping us from being appealing to the public," claimed frontman Chuck D, aka Carlton Ridenhour, their lead rapper, chief lyricist and marketing genius.

Chuck D's concept is based firmly on the belief that rhythm is king. "Rhythm, beat, soul... then next the lyrics and the meaning," he advocates. "If you don't have your funk in place then you are not going to get over to the masses of black people."

The Public Enemy stage show is the perfect vehicle to showcase their appeal. Dressed in combat gear with well staged manners and moves, they take the time to meet and shake hands with their audience. At an awards presentation at London's Royal Albert Hall, they wowed their hard core inveterates further by 'bum rushing' the stage and taking the microphone from dinner-jacketed Walter Stanton, inventor of the famous 'Stanton' scratch needs, for an impromptu performance of 'Rebel Without A Pause'. Bum-rushing is Public Enemy speak for gatecrashing.

A design graduate, Chuck D already had ten years experience as DJ, rap-show poster designer and hip-hop promoter. He knew what the hip-hop market wanted and together with co-producers Bill Stephney of Def Jam, Hank Shocklee, MC Flavor-Flav and DJ Terminator X, the most outwardly militant member of the crew, he loaded his vocal Uzi and fired: "My Uzi is my mouth and the bullets are the words I speak."

The way in which the beats and rhythms are crafted around important social issues has earned them titles such as "the genre's newest cultural terrorists" and "the black panthers of rap", not to mention the award for the best hip-hop record of 1987 at the Disco Mix Club World Finals during the spring of '88.

Public Enemy's first album 'Yo! Bum Rush The Show', released by Def Jam in 1987 sold over 300,000 copies in the US while their second 'It Takes A Nation Of Millions To Hold Us Back' sold three times as many. Def Jam confidently expect the third to move upwards into telephone number territory.

Chuck D claims that being a rapper is like being a public enemy these days. "People come gunning for you," he says – hence the group's name. With rap activists such as NWA now stirring the muddy waters of Hip-hop, Public Enemy face stiff competition in the preaching stakes. They may well have to drop the Uzi and find a more powerful weapon if they are to gun their way to similar success in the nineties.

"I am the public enemy but I don't rob banks. I don't fire bullets but I don't fire blanks. If my Uzi wasn't heavy I'd probably fire it. Make you walk the plank if I was a pirate. The level of rap has never been thinner. It's a runaway race, where I'm the winner," raps Chuck D in Miuzi Weighs A Ton.

There's a confidence there with which few could argue.

YO! BUM RUSH THE SHOW

PUBLIC
ENEMY
YO! BUM RUSH THE SHOW
RNMENT'S RESPONSIBLE...THE GOVERNMENT'S RESPONSIBLE...THE GOVERNMENT'S RESPONSIBLE......THE GOVERNMENT'S RESPONSIBLE... THE GOVERNMENT'S RESPONSIBLE......THE GOV

SOPHISTICATED

That women in the corner cold playin' the role
Just leave her ass in the corner till her feet get cold
Knowin' for a fact – that girl is whacked
If you hold your hand out she'll turn her back
Better walk, don't talk – she's all pretend
Can't be her friend unless you spend
Wall to wall – after all
Get ready to throw only money at the bitch

(chorus) Cause she thinks she's sophisticated

Peekin', seekin' inside a book
Her demands for a man with a chemical look
Wishes, desires – gettin' worse with age
She doesn't want a man – all she wants is a page
Ain't got no man so she goes to a club
Blacks think it's classy but it's really a pub
But that's the kind of place she likes to go
The bitch got a problem

(repeat chorus)

Jackets, shoes, everyday ties
The girl only wants one of those guys
Suckers who front like it ain't no thing
Pretend to be friends – don't want that thang
Talk like this – don't talk slang
Do anything to get that thang
Tries to be chic and play it off
Peekin' through the window – I saw her take her clothes off
Nasty girl – stone cold freak
Stayin' in bed a whole goddamn week
Comin' and leavin' – guys servin' up storms
From execs with checks – boys from the dorms
Never kept a name – never seen a face
She could pass 'em in the street like it never took place
I know she's a ho so I'm a go expose the funky bitch

(repeat chorus)

Now she wants a sucker but with an attache
And if you ain't got it – she'll turn you away
You can smile with style but you lost your trial
Cause you got a gold tooth – she thinks you're wild
She don't want a brother that's true and black
If you're light, you're alright – better stay back
Cause the sucker with the bag is out the catch
With something in his bag keepin' her attached
The man's got a plan – it's IBM
The devil at her level – yes it's him
His Audi – she rides hid gold and clothes
The ill base method – turning up her nose
Lack a lack a lack – now beaming her up
She still got the nerve to turn her funky nose up
Her status look at us from down below
Now the bitch is in trouble

(repeat chorus)

Little is known about her past
So listen to me cause I know her ass
Used to steal money out her boyfriend's clothes
And never got caught so the story goes
She kept doin' that to all her men
Found the wrong man when she did it again
And still to this day people wonder why
He didn't beat the bitch down till she almost died

Sophisticated

© Copyright 1987 by
Def American Songs (BMI).
All Rights Reserved.
International Copyright Secured.

BITCH

⑨

Lyrics by
W. Drayton,
C. Ridenhour,
and
H. Shocklee

Music by
C. Ridenhour
and
H. Shocklee

sophisticated

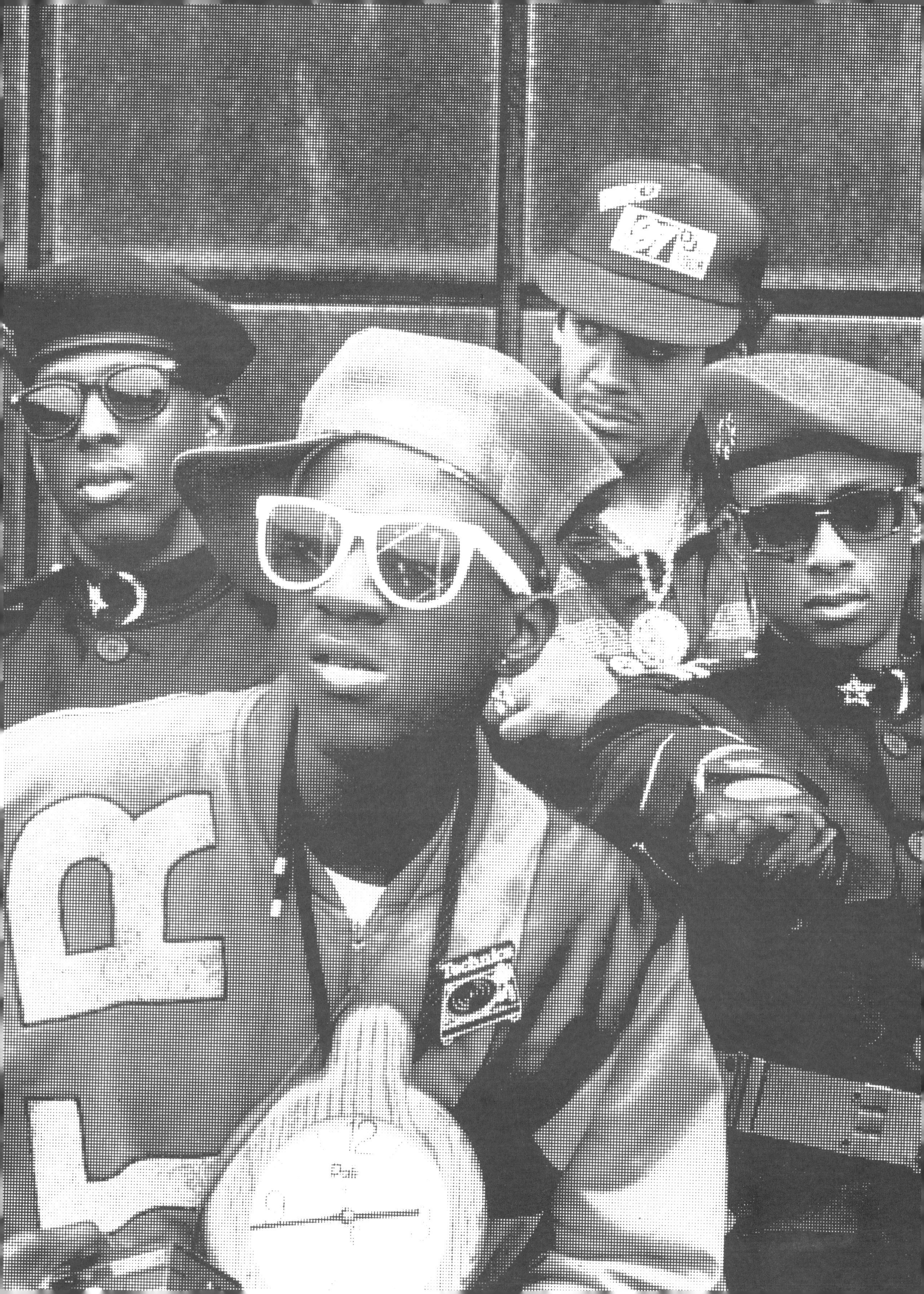

MIUZI WEIGHS A TON

Music and lyrics by C. Ridenhour and H. Shocklee

© Copyright 1987 by Def American Songs (BMI).
All Rights Reserved.
International Copyright Secured.

Step back, get away – give the borther some room
You got to turn me up when the beat goes boom
Lyric to lyric – line to line
Then you'll understand my reputation for rhyme
Cause my rhyme reputation depends on what
Style of record my DJ cuts
His slice, dice – super mix so nice
So bad you won't dispute the price
It's plain to see – it's a strain to be
Number one in the public eye enemy
I'm wanted in fifty – almost fifty-one
States where the posse got me on the run
It's a big wonder why I haven't gone under
Dodgin' all types of microphone thunder
A fugitive missin' all types of hell
All this because I talk so well – when I

(chorus) Rock – get up – get down
Miuzi weighs a ton

The match up title – the expression of thrill
For elite to compete and attempt to get ill
If looks could kill – I'd chill until
The public catches on to my material
Ducks criticize my every phase rapture
Can't wait to read the headlines of my capture
Accused of assault – a first degree crime
Cause I beat competitors with my rhymes
Tongue whipped, pushed, shoved, and tripped
Choked from the hold of my Kung Fu grip
And if you want my title it would be suicidal
From my end it would be homicidal
When I do work you get destroyed
Make all paranoid – try to avoid
The Public Enemy seat I've enjoyed
This is no kid and I'm not no toy boy

(repeat chorus)

I'm a Public Enemy but I don't rob banks
I don't shoot bullets and I don't shoot blanks
My style is supreme – number one is my rank
And I got more power than the New York Yanks
If miuzi wasn't heavy I'd probably fire it
I'd make you walk the plank if I was a pirate
If they made me a king – I would be a tyrant
If you want to get me – go ahead and try it
Snatcher, dispatcher, biter never been a
Instead of takin' me out – take a girl to dinner
The level of comp has never been thinner
It's a runaway race where I'm the winner
It's unreal – they call the law
And claimed I had started a war
It was war they wanted and war they got
But they wilted in the heat when miuzi got hot

(repeat chorus)

My style versatile said without rhymes
Which is why they're after me on my back
Lookin' over my shoulder – seein' what I write
Hearin' what I say – then wonderin' why
Why they can't ever compete on my level
Superstar status is my domain
Understand my rhythm – my pattern of lecture
And then you'll know why I'm on the run
This change of events results in a switch
Lateral movements of my vocal pitch
It eliminates pressure on the haunted
But the posse is around so I got to front it
Plus employ tactics so coy
And leave no choice but to destroy
Soloists, groups and what they say
And all that try to cross my way

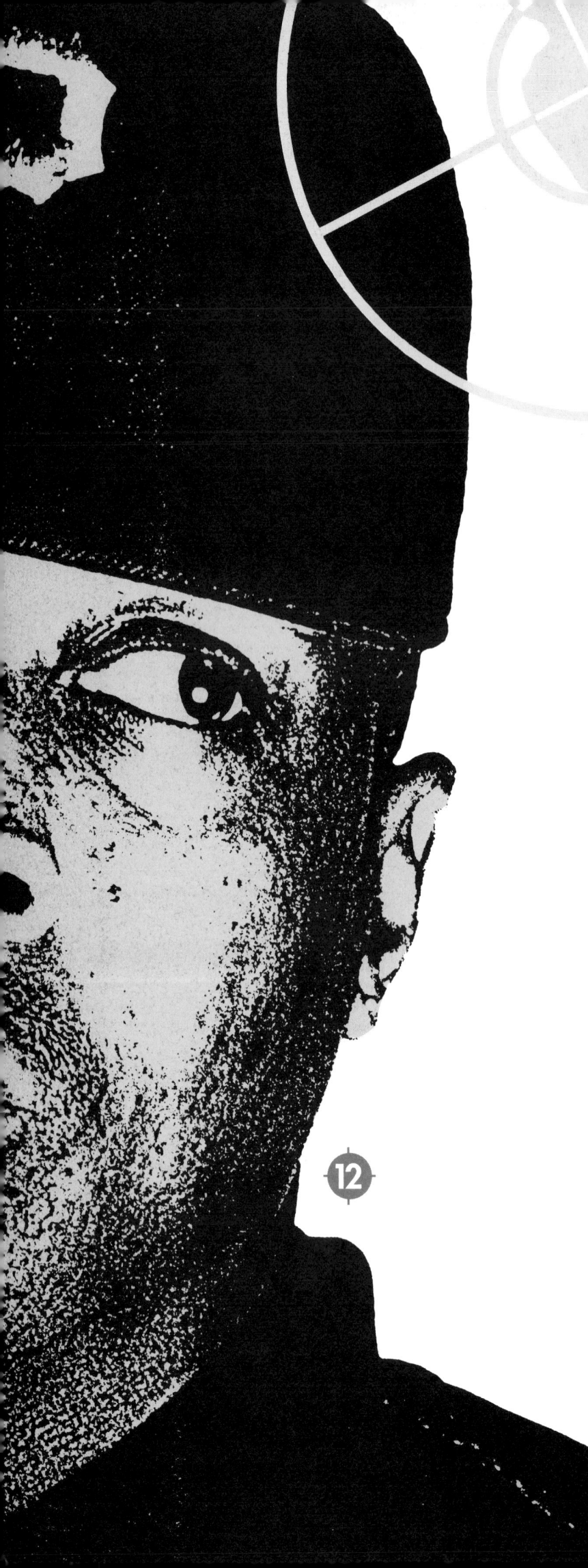

Music and lyrics by C. Ridenhour and H. Shocklee

You go ooh and ahh when I jump in my car
People treat me like Kareem Abdul Jabbar
No matter who you are – I'm up to par
I betcha go hip hop, hooray, hurrah
But the ahhs and ohhs is my kind of news
Pop your tape in – put your car in cruise
I never heard the boos – I never drank booze
Cause I just rock the rhythm – let alone the blues
The L.I. mystique – you sneak to peek
A look and then you know that we're ever weak
I know you can't wait – it's never too late
No fear, I'm here and everything is straight
Cycles, cycles – life runs in cycles
New is old – no I'm not no psycho
The monkey on the back makes the best excel
The people in the crowd makes the best rock well
The people in the back let you know who's whack
And those who lack the odds are stacked
The one who makes the money in white not black
You might not believe it but it's like that
When you come to my show – watch me throw
Down with the other brothers toe to toe
When you make a move – new not used
And watch the bro here just bust a groove
A fat lady soprano loads my ammo
And hear my jam with a funky piano
Easy on the wall but hard on the panel
A fool smokes Kool's cause he chokes on Camels
In effect – the crew's in check
Run by the posse with the gold around the neck
Homeboys in heat – lookin' for sweet
Ladies in the crowd so they can meet
Somebody to body – makin' a baby

TIMEBOMB

Givin' it to Gramdma then makin' her crazy
I'm a M.C. protector – U.S. defector
South African government wrecker
Panther power – you can feel it in my arm
Lookout y'all cause I'm a timebomb
Tickin', tockin', all about rockin'
Makin' much dollars while the crazy one's clockin'
The rhythm to shake the house downy down
Bounce to ounce – sound to crown
The man, the enemy, Public King – no
All fall to the force on my swing
Like Ali-Frazier Thriller in Manila
A pinpoint, point blank microphone killer am I
No need to lie – got the Flavor-flave
To prove ill win and if not – the save
I'll pick up, rack up – put your whole shack up
Just choose to lose the bet – M.C. stick up
This is the wiz but the mike's not his, it's mine
One time let the star shine
And I'm tellin' you – yelling at you you're through
Don't think you're grown because your moustache grew
I'm number one – you know it weighs a ton
And I'll be the burger – you can be the bun, girl
Surroundin' – my steady poundin'
Get – get on down to my funky sound
And rock the rhythm rhyme – one time your mind
Rhythm roll – two times control
The mauler and the caller of your doom
And when I'm ready to leave – your gonna know I go boom
Three times y'all – rhythm rhyme and rock
Then you'll know that the D. is on the block
Four times y'all and never ever the whack
It's the hour to the minute – time to blow BLACK

© Copyright 1987 by Def American Songs (BMI).
All Rights Reserved. International Copyright Secured.

BUM RUSH THE SHOW

I am taking no prisoners – taking no shorts
Breakin' with the metal of couple of forts
While we're hearin' that boom supplement the mix
We're gonna rush 'em like the Bears in the '46
Homeboys I don't know but they're part of the pack
In the plan against the man – bum rush attack
For the suckers at the door – if you're up and around
For the suckers at the door – we're gonna knock you down

(chorus) Yo! Bum rush the show!

Searchin' my body for fuckin' what?
Cause my gun shoots for fun and my knife don't cut
How can I you understand
I get ill on a posse with my goddam hands
Troubles – not me – I don't mean to cause
But you took one look and began to pause
Didn't hollar at the dollar we was willin' to spend
But you took one look and wouldn't let our ass in

(repeat chorus)

Cold bum rushin' doors like at first it's something
But all we realize that the show ain't nothin'
For the stunts and the blunts – whole world inside
The reason that the mighty used force supplied
No comp – we'll stomp all in our way
Gave me static so I won't pay
It might be a trick that you don't like
Comin' in the side door then grabbin' the mike
Walkin' and talkin' – fist full in the air
It might seem like that we don't care
A ho for an oh – a pow for an ow
Girls start screamin – all I say is wow
Get that sucker who shot that gun
Beat his monkey ass till it ain't no fun
5-0 showed and wouldn't you know
They blamed it on the kid cause all I said was . . .

(repeat chorus)

Lyrics by
W. Drayton,
C. Ridenhour,
and H. Shocklee

Music by
C. Ridenhour and
H. Shocklee

© Copyright 1987 by Def American Songs Inc. (BMI).
All Rights Reserved. International Copyright Secured.

MEGA-BLAST

Lyrics by W. Drayton, C. Ridenhour, and H. Shocklee
Music by C. Ridenhour and H. Shocklee

Time is gettin' crazy – people clockin' out
They're robbin' all the cribs ona death wish route
Breakin' into cars trying to steal their system
20 pounds on the bar – betcha can't lift 'em
Ya throw two punches – now you got no wind
Hittin' mega pipes – gettin' super stupid thin
Crying all the tears – smokin' all the squares
Workin' for ya boy – ya came short and full of swears
Ya couldn't make the money cause ya smoked up all the product
Walkin' round the town – skeptalepsy illaroduct
Can't be trusted cause you're living in the past
Ya should have kept ya ass away from that blast

Mega-Blast

I got a homeboy who is out on the block
He sells more crack than they sell fish at the dock
He runs to every car – thinking he's a star
He gets his product snatched by some people in the car
The car pulls off – he hung onto the side
Of the car that is in motion – guess his product took a ride
He tried to sell a dime for a thirty dollar bill
Fake gold plate on the back – no frill
Fake Hawaiian suit – scratched up knees
In his fridgerator – bread, water, cheese
Antique fork – how long will it last?
We'll see in twelve minutes when he wants that blast

© Copyright 1987 by Def American Songs Inc. (ASCAP). All Rights Reserved. International Copyright Secured.

TOO MUCH POSSE

What do you got to say about this
A force so strong you can't resist
You may as well join 'em – you know you can't beat 'em
Pack a hundred people – ya know ya gonna need 'em
Straight with the system is down by law
Cause every two hours they get nine more
They run all the dollars that come in town
Either join the crew or get beat down
I watched all the guys be so damn cruel
Try to get fast – you must be a fool
Blood through and through – the boys don't play
I seen 'em tax and run an operation today
They got too, too, too much posse

Yeah, I threw a party – much people came by
I'm talking to a 'g' cause the 'g' real fly
Sittin' in my room – chewin' off my ear
Chillin' stupid fly – I got stupid gear
My door kicked open – her man and crew
The 'g' turned to me and said, "Who you?"
So I said, "Yo fly, yeah the 'g' lied."
Stuck in the corner while the 'g' cried
And then from the back – my homeboys came
He pulled out a gun and said, "Go blame."
Ya lying ass girl with the fake tears
We got a posse and we show no fears
We got too, too, too much posse

© Copyright 1987 by Def American Songs (BMI).
All Rights Reserved. International Copyright Secured.

Music by C. Ridenhour and H. Shocklee
Lyrics by W. Drayton, C. Ridenhour, and H. Shocklee

PUBLIC

ENEMY #1

Well I'm all in – put it up on the board
Another rapper shot down from the mouth that roared
1-2-3 down for the count
The result of my lyrics – oh yes, no doubt
Cold rock rap – 49er supreme
Is what I choose and I use – I never lose to a team
Cause I can go solo like a sugar ray bolo
Make the fly girls wanna have my photo
Run in their room – hang it up on the wall
In remembrance that I rocked them all
Suckers, ducks, ho-hum Mc's
You can't beat the kid so go cut the cheese
Take this application of rhymes like these
My rap's red hot – 110 degrees
So don't start bassin' cause ill start placin'
Bets on that you'll be disgracing
You and your mind from a beatin' from my rhymes
A time, a crime that I can't find
I'll show you my gun – miuzzi weighs a ton
Because I'm public enemy number one

You got no rap but you want to battle
It's like having a boat – but you got no paddle
Cause I never pause – I say it because
I don't break in stores – I break all laws
Written while sittin' – all fittin', not bitten
Givin' me the juice that you're not gettin'
I'm not a law obeyer – so you can tell your mayor
I'm a non-stop, rhythm rock poetry sayer
I'm the rhyme player – the ozone layer
A battle, what? – here's a bible so start you're prayer
A word to the wise is justified
If they ask you happened – just admit you lied
You just got caught – for going out of order
And now you're servin' football teams their water
You just got dissed – all but dismissed
Sucker duck Mc's – you get me pissed
It's no fun being on the run
Cause they got me – public enemy number one

For all you suckers, liars – your cheap amplifiers
Your crossed up wires are always starting fires
For you grown up criers – now here's a pair of pliers
Get a job like your mother – I heard she fixes old tires
You try to sell ya equipment – but you get no buyers
It's you they never hire – you're never on flyers
Cause you a you're crew is only known as good triers
Known as the poetic lyrical son
I'm public enemy number one

Music and Lyrics by C. Ridenhour and H. Shocklee

© Copyright 1987 by Def American Songs (BMI).
All Rights Reserved. International Copyright Secured.

Music and Lyrics by C. Ridenhour and H. Shocklee

You spend a buck in the 80's – what you get is a preacher
Forgivin' this torture of the system that brought 'cha
I'm a mission and you got that right
Addin' fuel to the fire – punch to the fight
Many have forgotten what we came hear for
Never knew or had a clue so you're on the floor
Just growin, not knowin' about your past
Now you're lookin' pretty stupid while you're shakin' your ass

(chorus) Mind over matter – mouth in motion
Can't deny it cause I'll never be quiet
Let's start this right

Some people fear me when I walk this way
Some come near me – some run away
Some people take head to every word I say
Some wanna build a posse – some stay away
Some people think that we plan to fail
Wonder why we go under or go to jail
Some ask us why we act the way we act
Without lookin' how long they kept us back

(repeat chorus)

Yes if I bore you – I won't ignore you
I'm sayin' things that they say I'm not supposed to
Give you pride that you may not find
If you're blind about your past then ill point behind
Kings, queens, warriors, lovers
People proud – sisters and brothers
It's the biggest fear – suckers get tears
When we can top their best idea

(repeat chorus)

Our solution – mind revolution
Can't sell it – no you can't buy it in a potion
You lie about the life that you wanted to try
Tellin' me about a head you wanted to fly
Another brother with the same woes that you face
But you shot with the same hands – you fali from grace
Every brother should be every brother's keeper
But you shot with your left while your right was on your beeper

(repeat chorus)

As the world turns – it's a terrible waste
To see the stupid look stuck on your face
Timebomb alarm for the world – just try it
Known to all zones as the one man riot
I'm on a mission to set you straight
Children it's not too late
Explain to the world when it's plain to see
To be what the world doesn't want us to be

(repeat chorus)

© Copyright 1987 by Def American Songs (BMI).
All Rights Reserved. International Copyright Secured.

RIGHT STARTER

M.P.E.

I'm cold gettin' busy while I'm shakin' you down
I'm on the air – you're on the ground
Cuck D. – the enemy – words you heed
Built for speed – but what you need is
Funky fresh lyrics fallin' down on time
Your enemy poppin' it – droppin' a dime
Comin' back rockin' a tomahawk slam
And still gettin' fly with the mike in my hand
I'm cold coolin' out – laying in the shade
Dealers buggin' cause they're gonna get sprayed
Their intimidator – your Scarface
What's goin' on (huh) what's taking place
I don't wear gold but I clock ducats
And I have the money overflowing out of buckets
You want crazy dollars – I make people hollar
You stick 'em up stupid and I'm snatching biters collars

I'll rebuild the mind to alleviate
Unnecessary pressures that can recreate
The sting that stung Yama-Goochie Foo Yung
When he bit the Public Enemy he only got hung
Cause his brain was gettin' bigger than a pregnant toad
His heartbeat stopped cause of overload
I made the beat that broke his back
I cut his circulation – made his world turn black
I find out things like E.S.P.
Amazing world of Kreskin's brain velocity
Like Alexander Mundy – I'm in like Flynt
Mercedes limousine with a hardcore tint
I'm captain of the ship – I make them walk the planks
Riding around the world – hundred sixty million francs
Not like the kind that you put on the grill
Cause I only do it like that when I'm on chill hill

I'm going for the money that man never made
Gettin' thrill from orders – suckers obeyed
It's gettin' late and I can't wait
To drive by the bus and rock my tape
My car is movin' fast – like a train
Never skid off the road – even in the rain
Cold dodgin' tickets – rockin' all the jams
Make biters step back and understand
When I got to the beach – the ground's so sandy
Girls on my jock like ants on candy
Checking out the fellas with their girls on the side
Put ya boat in the water – let's take a ride
To the land of party people – rocking, shocking to the beat
So keep ya eyes on ya girl cause you know I'm gonna cheat
I'm gonna max and relax and chill my will
Body rockin', brain shockin' makes your heart stand still

Lyrics by W. Drayton, C. Ridenhour, and H. Shocklee

Music by C. Ridenhour and H. Shocklee

© Copyright 1987 by Def American Songs (BMI).
All Rights Reserved. International Copyright Secured.

(chorus)
Raise your hands – so we can
Raise the roof – so you can
Raise your voice – so we can
Raise the roof

Raise the roof because it's all on fire
Not done by the sun or electrical wire
Not done by sons striking matching with daughters
But done by scratches so save the water
This jam is packed so I just figure
All we need is the house to get bigger
So startin' with the roof down to the base
We're at your service to burn the place

(repeat chorus)

With the spot as hot as it can get
The roof's on fire – you're soaked and wet
The puzzle on your face shows you as sweat
But your body keeps movin' with no regret
Chandeliers shake – swing from front to back
Left to right all night – and the lights don't crack
Your minds on the time – hopin' it don't end
It's time to get stupid – here we go again

(repeat chorus)

Stare at the strobe – pull yor earlobe
For the sights and sounds clear across the globe
This jam might hit or miss the charts
But the style gets wild as state of the art
Dazzling in science – bold in nerve
But givin' by house what it deserves
Served on the floor cause I got paid
Make the fans that left – wish they had'a stayed
Realize my friend – ain't this a trip
As your body gets railed when you do the flip
And your mind gets rocked when we're on a roll
Then the freak of the week makes you lose control
A Swatch for a watch – so you'll know the time
Your crowd gets loud and you clock my rhyme
The messiah's on fire and I'm living proof
I'll quench your desire and raise your roof

(repeat chorus)

In school I'm cool throughout the week
When the weekend comes – I'm down with the Greeks
Frat brothers known across the seven seas
Fly ladies of the 80's – sororities
Zeltas, Deltas, AKA's
Women that keep me in a daze
A-Phi-A – Sigma boys on the move
With the Kappas and the Ques and of course the grooves to

Raise the roof

And for real it's the deal and the actual fact
Takes a nation of millions to hold me back
Rejected and accepted as a communist
Claimin' fame to my name as a terrorist
Makin' money in corners that you'll never see
Dodgin' judges and the lawyers and the third degree
Nothin' wrong with a song to make the strong survive
Realize gave me five cause I kept 'em alive
Mislead what you read 'bout my devilish deeds
Mislead what I said so you're better off dead
Make 'em hear it and see it for the Def and blind
And command it and we'll plan it for incapable minds
Take for granted and demand it from the wave of my hand
Make the jealous understand it – just say damn
When they see me ask a question – "How the Hell can it be?"
When they watch me pull a serpent straight out of the sea
Turn the winter into summer – then from hot to cold
Expand my power on the hour – make you all behold
From the slammer swing a hammer like the mighty Thor
God of thunder, you'll go under – then you'll all applaud
And fathom that distance – the mad must reap
Meet Namor sea lord – Prince of deep
Here for you to fear at any cost
Tellin' you to get busy or you better get lost
Livin' lives civilized from the lessons I taught
Cities buried underground just because I went off
My friends, enemies – better by my friend
Is question people guessin' is this the end?

End of the world – are you guessin' yes?
Just say don't delay it – get it off your chest
Houses of crack – I've seen too much
I go ready – aim – fire – then I'll blow 'em up

Lyrics by
C. Ridenhour and
H. Shocklee

Music by
C. Ridenhour,
E. Sadler and
H. Shocklee

RAISE THE ROOF

IT TAKES A NA[TION]
OF MILLION[S TO]
HOLD US [BACK]

PUBLIC
ENEMY
IT
TAKES
A
NATION
OF
MILLIONS
TO
FREEDOM IS A ROAD SELDOM TRAVELED BY THE MULTITUDE . . . FREEDOM IS A ROAD SELDOM TRAVELED BY THE MULTITUDE . . . FREEDOM IS A ROAD SELDOM TRAVELED BY THE MULTITUDE . . .

BRING THE NOISE

By Carlton Ridenhour, Eric Sadler

Bass! How low can you go?
Death row. What a brother knows.
Once again, back is the incredible
the rhyme animal
the incredible D, Public Enemy Number One
"Five-O" said, "Freeze!" and I got numb
Can I tell 'em that I really never had a gun?
But it's the wax that the Terminator X spun
Now they got me in a cell 'cause my records, they sell
'Cause a brother like me said, "Well...
...Farrakhan's a prophet and I think you ought to listen to
what he can say to you, what you ought to do."
Follow for now, power of the people, say,
"Make a miracle, D, pump the lyrical"
Black is back, all in, we're gonna win
Check it out, yeah y'all, here we go again

Chorus: Turn it up! Bring the noise!

Never badder than bad 'cause the brother is madder than mad
At the fact that's corrupt as a senator
Soul on a roll, but you treat it like soap on a rope
'Cause the beats in the lines are so dope
Listen for lessons I'm saying inside music that the critics are blasting me for
They'll never care for the brothers and sisters now across the country has us up for the war

We got to demonstrate, come on now, they're gonna have to wait
Till we get it right
Radio stations I question their blackness
They call themselves black, but we'll see if they'll play this

Chorus: Turn it up! Bring the noise!

© Copyright 1987. Lyrics reproduced by permission of Island Music Limited.
All Rights Reserved. International Copyright Secured.

& Hank Shocklee

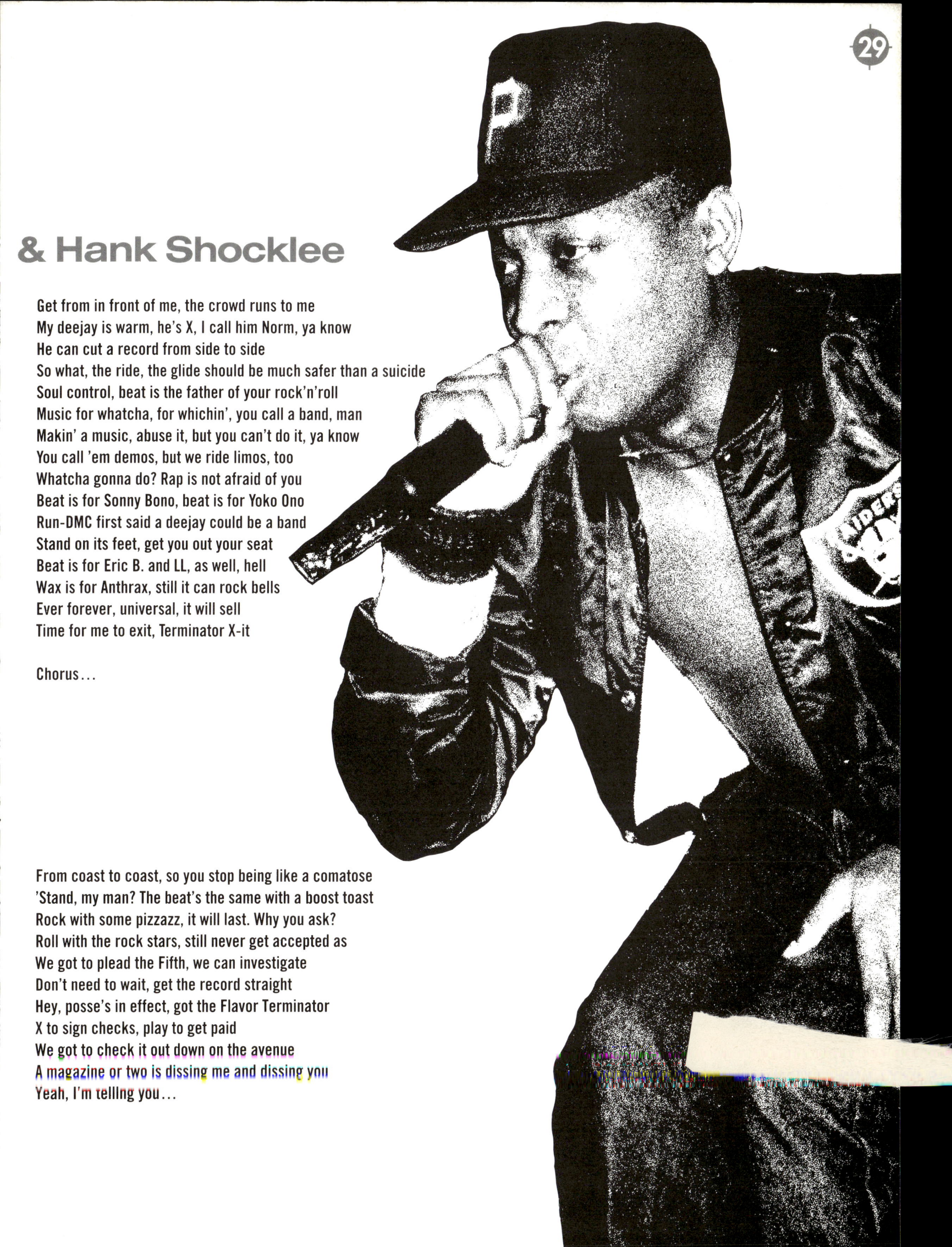

Get from in front of me, the crowd runs to me
My deejay is warm, he's X, I call him Norm, ya know
He can cut a record from side to side
So what, the ride, the glide should be much safer than a suicide
Soul control, beat is the father of your rock'n'roll
Music for whatcha, for whichin', you call a band, man
Makin' a music, abuse it, but you can't do it, ya know
You call 'em demos, but we ride limos, too
Whatcha gonna do? Rap is not afraid of you
Beat is for Sonny Bono, beat is for Yoko Ono
Run-DMC first said a deejay could be a band
Stand on its feet, get you out your seat
Beat is for Eric B. and LL, as well, hell
Wax is for Anthrax, still it can rock bells
Ever forever, universal, it will sell
Time for me to exit, Terminator X-it

Chorus…

From coast to coast, so you stop being like a comatose
'Stand, my man? The beat's the same with a boost toast
Rock with some pizzazz, it will last. Why you ask?
Roll with the rock stars, still never get accepted as
We got to plead the Fifth, we can investigate
Don't need to wait, get the record straight
Hey, posse's in effect, got the Flavor Terminator
X to sign checks, play to get paid
We got to check it out down on the avenue
A magazine or two is dissing me and dissing you
Yeah, I'm telling you…

Back
Caught you lookin' for the same thing
It's a new thing – check out this I bring
Uh Oh the roll below the level
'Cause I'm livin' low next to the bass, C'mon
Turn up the radio
They claim that I'm a criminal
By now I wonder how
Some people never know
The enemy could be their friend, guardian
I'm not a hooligan
I rock the party and
Clear all the madness, I'm not a racist
Preach to teach to all
'Cause some they never had this
Number one, not born to run
About the gun…
I wasn't licensed to have one
The minute they see me, fear me
I'm the epitome – a public enemy
Used, abused without clues
I refused to blow a fuse
They even had it on the news
Don't believe the hype…

Yes
Was the start of my last jam
So here it is again, another def jam
But since I gave you all a little something
That we knew you lacked
They still consider me a new jack
All the critics you can hang 'em
I'll hold the rope
But they hope to the pope
And pray it ain't dope
The follower of Farrakhan
Don't tell me that you understand
Until you hear the man
The book of the new school rap game
Writers treat me like Coltrane, insane
Yes to them, but to me I'm a different kind
We're brothers of the same mind, unblind
Caught in the middle and
Not surrenderin'
I don't rhyme for the sake of riddlin'
Some claim that I'm a smuggler
Some say I never heard of 'ya
A rap burglar, false media
We don't need it do we?
It's fake that's what it be to 'ya, dig me?
Don't believe the hype…

Don't believe the hype – it's a sequel
As an equal, can I get this through to you
My 98's boomin' with a trunk of funk
All the jealous punks can't stop the dunk
Comin' from the school of hard knocks
Some perpetrate, they drink Clorox
Attack the Black, cause I know they lack exact
The cold facts, and still they try to xerox
Leader of the new school, uncool
Never played the fool, just made the rules
Remember there's a need to get alarmed
Again I said I was a timebomb
In the daytime the radio's scared of me
'Cause I'm mad, plus I'm the enemy
They can't c'mon and play with me in primetime
'Cause I know the time, plus I'm gettin' mine
I get on the mix late in the night
They know I'm livin' right, so here go the mike, sike
Before I let it go, don't rush my show
You try to reach and grab and get elbowed
Word to Herb, yo if you can't swing this
Learn the words you might sing this
Just a little bit of the taste of the bass for you
As you get up and dance at the LQ
When some deny it, defy it I swing bolos
Then they clear the lane I go solo
The meaning of all of that
Some media is the whack
You believe it's true, it blows me through the roof
Suckers, liars get me a shovel
Some writers I know are damn devils
For them I say don't believe the hype
Yo Chuck, they must be on the pipe, right?
Their pens and pads I'll snatch
'Cause I've had it
I'm not an addict fiendin' for static
I'll see their tape recorder and grab it
No, you can't have it back silly rabbit
I'm goin' to my media assassin
Harry Allen, I gotta ask him
Yo Harry, you're a writer, are we that type?
Don't believe the hype
I got Flavor and all those things you know
Yeah boy, part two bum rush and show
Yo Griff, get the green black red and
Gold down countdown to Armageddon
'88 you wait the Sls will
Rock the hard jams – treat it like a seminar
Teach the bourgeoise, and rock the boulevard
Some say I'm negative
But they're not positive
But what I got to give…
The media says this

By Carlton Ridenhour, Eric Sadler & Hank Shocklee

DON'T BELIEVE THE HYPE

FLAVOR FLAV

By W. Drayton, Eric Sadler & Hank Shocklee

Um lampin, um lampin, um cole cole lampin
I got loowies boy, um not trampin
I just came from Da-crib ya know
Um on da go – throw ya tank into metro
Live lyrics from da bank of reality
I kick da flyest dope maneuver technicality
To a dope track, you wanna hike git out ya backpack
Um in my Flav-mobile cole lampin
I took dis g upstate cole campin
Ta da poke-a-nose, we call da hide-a-ways
A pack of franks and a big bag of frito lays

Flavor-Flav on a hype tip
Um ya hype drink, come take a big sip
Um in position, you can't play me out da pocket
I'll take da dopest beat you got and I'll rock-it
Like chocolate, even vanilla – chocolate, strawberry, saperella
Flavors are electric – try me – get a shock-a
Didn't I tell you to leave Flavor Flav alone knock-a
A clock on my chest proves I don't fess
I'm a clock-a, rock-a rockin' wit-da-rest
Flavor in da house by Chuck-D's side
Chuck got da Flavor-Flav don't hide
P.E. crazy, Crazy P.E. – makin' crazy loowies for the shoppin spree

Ya eatin death cause ya like gittin dirt from da graveyard – ya put gravy on it
Den ya pick ya teeth with tomb stone chips
And casket cover clips – dead women hips ya do da bump with – bones
Nutin but love bones
Lifestyles of da live-en-dead
First ya live den ya dead – died trying ta clock what I said
Now I got a murder rap cause I bust ya cap wit Flavor – pure Flavor

© Copyright 1988. Lyrics reproduced by permission of Island Music Limited. All Rights Reserved. International Copyright Secured.

COLD LAMPIN'

We got Magnum Brown, Shoothki-Valoothki
Super-calafraga-hestik-alagoothki
You could put dat in ya don't know what I said book
Took-look-yuk-duk-wuk
Shinavative ill factors by da Flavor Flav
Come an ride da Flavor wave
In any year on any givin day
What a brova know – what do Flavor say
Why do dis record play dat way
Prime time merrily in da day
Right now dis radio station is busy – brainknowledgeably wizzy
Honey drippers, you say you got it
You ain't got no flavor and I can prove it
Flavor Flav the flav of all flavors
Onion an garlic french fried potatoes
Make ya breath stink, breathe fire
Makes any onion da best crier

I know it sounds crazy but it fits perfect
Peter perfect pimped a perfect Peter
Honey dripper – sucker sipper – big dipper – sucker dripper
Drippin suckers like it's goin out-a-style
Creatin flavors for da Flavor Flav pile
Flavor Flav the flavor of da pile
Lampin booyee madina style

Kickin da flavor gittin busy
Ya goin ouut, I think ya dizzy
I think ya hungry, cause ya starvin fa Flavor
Flavor most, put it on ya toast
Eat it – en taste it en swallow it down
Imperial Flavor gives you da crown
Of the king called Flavor, da king of all flavors
Rolls an rolls an rolls of live savers
Flavor Flav is in everything ya eat cause everything ya eat got flavor
Flavor Flav is da first taste ya git in da mornin – ya breakfast is da flavor
In between dat ta lunch – in between dat dinner – in between dat ta midnight flavor
Yeah, das right I got somethin' fa all da fandangoes of damangoes of da fandangoes of da mangoes

TERMINATOR X
TO THE EDGE OF PANIC

Go, Go, Go, Go, Go, Go
Take a look at his style
Take a check of the sound
Off the record people keeping him down
Trick a chick in Miami
Terminator X packs the jams
Whow gives a fuck about Goddamn Grammy
Anyway and I say the D's defending the mike
Yeah, who gives a fuck about what they like
Right the power is bold, the rhymes politically cold
No judge can ever budge or ever handle his load
Yes the coming is near and he's about to become
The one and only missionary lord son of a gun
Going on and on back trackin' the whack
Explain the knack y'all for the actual fact, c'mon

Terminator X Go off (4X)
Go, Go, Go, Go, Go, Go

He goes on and on 'till he reaches the coast
Tired, wired of his own race playing him close
Understand his type of music kills the
Plan of the klan
You know the pack attack the man
With the palm of his hand
Police, wild beasts, dogs on a leash
No peace to reach-that's why he's packin' his black piece
Terminator X yellin' with his hands
Damn almighty rulin ready to jam
But his cuts drive against the belt
Sheet...he's bad by his damn self
Yeah, his one job cold threatens the crowd
The loud sound pound to make the brothers proud

Terminator X Go off (4X)
Go, Go, Go, Go, Go, Go

Gettin' small makin' room for it all
Flavors on the phone so he can...
Make the call
I know you're clockin' the enemy
You should be clockin' the time
Checkin' records I'm wreckin' you
For defecting my rhyme
No provokin', no jokin', you know the stage is set
If you're thinkin' I'm breakin'
He ain't rocked it yet
My education is takin' you for a long ride
I'll have you brain slip and do the slide
Glide into infinity, it's infinite
With your hands in your pockets
I know your money is spent
Like this, like that, butter for the fat
If you kill my dog, I'ma slay your cat
It's like that y'all, can you handle it son
I'm public enemy number one

Terminator X Go off (4X)
Go, Go, Go, Go, Go, Go

By Carlton Ridenhour, Norman Rogers & W. Drayton

© Copyright 1988. Lyrics reproduced by permission of Island Music Limited. All Rights Reserved. International Copyright Secured.

SHE WATCH CHANNEL ZERO?!

By Carlton Ridenhour, W. Drayton, Griffin, Eric Sadler & Hank Shocklee

The woman makes the men all pause
And if you got a woman
She might make you forget yours
There's a 5 letter word
To describe her character
But her brain's being washed by an actor
And every real man that tries to approach
Come the closer he comes
He gets dissed like a roach

REFRAIN:
I don't think I can handle
She goes channel to channel
Cold lookin' for that hero
She watch channel zero

CHORUS:
She watch, She watch 4X
(Flavor Ad lib)

2, 7, 5, 4, 8 she watched she said
All added up to zero
And nothing in her head
She turns and turns
And she hopes the soaps
Are for real – she learns
Is that it ain't true, nope
But she won't survive
And rather die and lie
Falls a fool – for some dude – on a tube

REPEAT REFRAIN
CHORUS

Trouble vision for a sister
Because I know she don't know, I quote
Her brains retrained
By a 24 inch remote
Revolution a solution
For all our children
But all her children
Don't mean as much as the show, I mean
Watch her worship the screen, and fiend
For a TV ad
And it just makes me mad

REPEAT REFRAIN
CHORUS

© Copyright 1988. Lyrics reproduced by permission of Island Music Limited. All Rights Reserved. International Copyright Secured.

LOUDER THAN A BOMB

This style seems wild
Wait before you treat me like a stepchild
Let me tell you why they got me on file
'Cause I give you what you lack
Come right and exact
Our status is the saddest
So I care where you at, black
And at home I got a call from Tony Rome
The FBI was tappin' my telephone
I never live alone
I never walk alone
My posses always ready, and they're waitin' in my zone
Although I live the life that of a resident
But I be knowin' the scheme that of the president
Tappin' my phone whose crews abused
I stand accused of doing harm
'Cause I'm louder than a bomb
C'mon C'mon louder etc…

I am the rock hard trooper
To the bone, the bone, the bone
Full grown – consider me – stone
Once again and
I say it for you to know
The troop is always ready, I yell 'geronimo'
Your CIA, you see I ain't kiddin'
Both King and X they got ridda' both
A story untold, true, but unknown
Professor Griff knows…
"I ain't milk toast"
And not the braggin' or boastin' and plus
It ain't no secret why they're tappin' my phone, although
I can't keep it a secret
So I decided to kick it, yo
And yes it weighs a ton
I say it once again
I'm called the enemy – I'll never be a friend
Of those with closed minds, don't know I'm rapid
The way that I rap it
Is makin' 'em tap it, yeah
Never servin' em well, 'cause I'm an un-Tom
It's no secret at all
Cause I'm louder than a bomb

Cold holdin' the load
The burden breakin' the mold
I ain't lyin', denyin', 'cause they're checkin' my code
Am I buggin' 'cause they're buggin' my phone – for information
No tellin' who's sellin' out – power buildin' the nation so…
Joinin' the set, the point blank target
Every brother's inside – so least not you forget, no
Takin' the blame is not a waste, here taste
A bit of the song so you can never be wrong
Just a bit of advice, 'cause we be payin' the price
'Cause every brother man's life
Is like swingin' the dice, right?
Here it is, once again this is
The brother to brother
The Terminator, the cutter

Goin' on an' on – leave alone the grown
Get it straight in '88, an' I'll troop it to demonstrate
The posse always ready – 98 at 98
My posse come quick, because my posse got velocity
Tappin' my phone, they never leave me alone
I'm even lethal when I'm unarmed
'Cause I'm louder than a bomb

'Cause the D is for dangerous
You can come and get some of this
I teach and speak
So when it's spoke, it's no joke
The voice of choice
The place shakes with bass
Called one for the treble
The rhythm is the rebel
Here's a funky rhyme that they're tappin' on
Just thinkin' I'm breakin' the beats I'm rappin' on
CIA FBI
All they tell us is lies
And when I say it they get alarmed
'Cause I'm louder than a bomb

By Carlton Ridenhour, Eric Sadler & Hank Shocklee

© Copyright 1988. Lyrics reproduced by permission of Island Music Limited.
All Rights Reserved. International Copyright Secured.

CAUGHT, CAN I G

By Carlton Ridenhour, Eric Sadler & Hank Shocklee

GET A WITNESS

© Copyright 1988. Lyrics reproduced by permission of Island Music Limited.
All Rights Reserved. International Copyright Secured.

Caught, now in court 'cause I stole a beat
This is a sampling sport
But I'm giving it a new name
What you hear is mine
P.E. you know the time
Now, what in the heaven does a jury know about hell
If I took it, but they just look at me
Like, Hey, I'm on a mission
I'm talkin' 'bout conditions
Ain't right sittin' like dynamite
Gonna blow you up and it just might
Blow up the bench and
Judge, the courtroom plus I gotta mention
This court is dismissed when I grab the mike
Yo Flave...What is this?

Get hyped, c'mon we gotta
Gather around – gotcha
Mail from the courts and jail
Claims I stole the beats that I rail
Look at how I'm livin' like
And they're gonna check the mike, right? – Sike
Look at how I'm livin' now, lower than low
What a sucker know
I found this mineral that I call a beat
I paid zero
I packed my load 'cause it's better than gold
People don't ask the price, but it's sold
They say that I sample, but they should
Sample this my pit bull
We ain't goin' for this
They say that I stole this
Can I get a witness?

Understand where we're goin'
Then listen to this, plus my Roland
Comin' from way down below
Rebound c'mon boost up the stereo
Snakes in the morning
Wake up, scared afraid of my warning
They claim that I'm violent
Now I choose to be silent
Can I get a witness?

C'mon get wit' it
Something ain't right, I got to admit it
Made me mad when I was on tour
That I declared war on black radio
They say that I planned this
On the radio most of you will demand this
Won't be on a playlist
Bust the way that I say this: No Sell Out

You singers are spineless
As you sing your senseless songs to the mindless
Your general subject love is minimal
It's sex for profit
Scream that I sample
For example, Tom you ran to the federal
Court in the U.S. it don't mean you
Yeah, 'cause they fronted on you
The posses ready, Terminator X yes he's ready
The S1W's, Griff are you ready?

They say that I stole this
I rebel with a raised fist, can we get a witness?

Here it is
BAMMM
And you say, Goddamn
This is the dope jam
But let's define the term called dope
And you think it mean funky now, no
Here is a true tale
Or the ones that deal
Are the ones that fail
Yeah
You can move if you wanna move
What it prove
It's here like the groove
The problem is this – we gotta' fix it
Check out the justice – and how they run it
Sellin', smellin'
Sniffin', riffin'
And brothers try to get swift an'
Sell to their own, rob a home
While some shrivel to bone
Like comatose walkin' around
Please don't confuse this with the sound
I'm talking about... BASS
I put this together to...
Rock the bells of those that
Boost the dose
Of lack a lack
And those that sell to Black
Shame on a brother when he dealin'
The same block where my 98 be wheelin'
And everybody know
Another kilo
From a corner from a brother to keep another –
Below
Stop illin' and killin'
Stop grillin'
Yo, black, yo (we are willin')
4, 5 o'clock in the mornin'
Wait a minute y'all
The fiends are fiendin'
Day to day they say no other way
This stuff...
Is really bad
I'm talkin' 'bout... BASS

Yo, listen
I see it on their faces
(First come first serve basis)
Standin' in line
Checkin' the time
Homeboys playin' the curb
The same ones that used to do herb
Now they're gone
Passin' it on
Poison attack – the Black word bond
Daddy-O
Once said to me
He knew a brother who stayed all day in his jeep
And at night he went to sleep
And in the mornin' all he had was
The sneakers on his feet
The culprit used to jam and rock the mike, yo
He stripped the jeep to fill his pipe
And wander around to find a place
Where they rocked to a different kind of... BASS

By Carlton Ridenhour, Eric Sadler & Hank Shocklee

© Copyright 1988.
Lyrics reproduced by permission of
Island Music Limited.
All Rights Reserved.
International Copyright Secured.

NIGHT OF THE LIV

ING BASSHEADS

BLACK STEEL IN THE HOUR OF CHAOS

By Carlton Ridenhour, W. Drayton, Eric Sadler & Hank Shocklee

I got a letter from the government
The other day
I opened and read it
It said they were suckers
They wanted me for their army or whatever
Picture me givin' a damn – I said never
Here is a land that never gave a damn
About a brother like me and myself
Because they never did
I wasn't wit' it, but just that very minute
It occurred to me
The suckers had authority
Cold sweatin' as I dwell in my cell
How long has it been?
They got me sittin' in the state pen
I gotta get out – but that thought was thought before
I contemplated a plan on the cell floor
I'm not a fugitive on the run
But a brother like me begun – to be another one
Public enemy servin' time – they drew the line y'all
To criticize me some crime – never the less
They could not understand that I'm a Black man
And I could never be a veteran
On the strength, the situation's unreal
I got a raw deal, so I'm goin' for the steel

They got me rottin' in the time that I'm servin'
Tellin' you what happened the same time they're throwin'
4 of us packed in a cell like slaves – oh well
The same motherfucker got us livin' in his hell
You have to realize – what it's a form of slavery
Organized under a swarm of devils
Straight up – word 'em up on the level
The reasons are several, most of them federal
Here is my plan anyway and I say
I got gusto, but only some I can trust – Yo
Some do a bid from 1 to 10
And I never did, and plus I never been
I'm on a tier where no tears should ever fall
Cell block and locked – I never clock it y'all
'Cause time and time again time
They got me servin' to those and to them
I'm not a citizen
But even when I catch a C-O
Sleepin' on the job – my plan is on go-ahead
On the strength, I'm a tell you the deal
I got nothin' to lose
'Cause I'm goin' for the steel

© Copyright 1988. Lyrics reproduced by permission of Island Music Limited.
All Rights Reserved. International Copyright Secured.

You know I caught a C-O
Fallin' asleep on death row
I grabbed his gun – then he did what I said so
And everyman's got served
Along with the time they served
Decency was deserved
To understand my demands
I gave a warnin' – I wanted the governor, y'all
And plus the warden to know
That I was innocent –
Because I'm militant
Posing a threat, you bet it's fuckin' up the government
My plan said I had to get out and break north
Just like with Oliver's neck
I had to get off – my boys had the feds in check
They couldn't try nuthin'
We had a force to instigate a prison riot
This is what it takes for peace
So I just took the piece
Black for Black inside time to cut the leash
Freedom to get out – to the ghetto – no sell out
6 C-O's we got we ought put their head out
But I'll give 'em a chance, cause I'm civilized
As for the rest of the world, they can't realize
A cell is hell – I'm a rebel so I rebel
Between bars, got me thinkin' like an animal
Got a woman C-O to call me a copter
She tried to get away, and I popped her
Twice, right
Now who wanna get nice?
I had 6 C-O's, now it's 5 to go
And I'm serious – call me delirious
But I'm still a captive
I gotta rap this
Time to break as time grows intense
I got the steel in my right hand
Now I'm lookin' for the fence

I ventured into the courtyard
Followed by 52 brothers
Bruised, battered, and scarred but hard
Goin' out with a bang
Ready to bang out
But power from the sky
And from the tower shots rang out
A high number in dose – yes
And some came close
Figure I trigger my steel
Stand and hold my post
This is what I mean – an anti-nigger machine
If I come out alive and then they won't – come clean
And then I threw up my steel bullets – flew up
Blew up, who shot...
What, who, the bazooka was who
And to my rescue, it was the S1W's
Secured my getaway, so I just got away
The joint broke, from the black smoke
Then they saw it was rougher than the average bluffer
'Cause the steel was black, the attitude exact
Now the chase is on tellin' you to c'mon
53 brothers on the run and we are gone

© Copyright 1988. Lyrics reproduced by permission of Island Music Limited. All Rights Reserved. International Copyright Secured.

REBEL WITHOUT A PAUSE

By Carlton Ridenhour,
Norman Rogers,
Eric Sadler
& Hank Shocklee

Yes-the rhythm, the rebel
Without a pause – I'm lowering my level
The hard rhymer – where you never been I'm in
You want stylin' – you know it's time again
D the enemy – tellin' you to hear it
They praised the music – this time they play the lyrics
Some say no to the album, the show
Bum rush the sound I made a year ago
I guess you know – you guess I'm just a radical
Not on sabbatical – yes to make it critical
The only part your body should be parting to
Panther power on the hour from the rebel to you

Radio – suckers never play me
On the mix – just O.K. me
Not known and grown when they're clocking my zone
  it's known
Snakin' and takin' everything that a brother owns
Hard – my calling card
Recorded and ordered – supporter of Chesimard
Loud and proud kickin' live next poet supreme
Loop a troop, bazooka, the scheme
Flavor – a rebel in his own mind
Supporter of my rhyme
Designed to scatter a line of suckers who claim I do crime
They're on my time

   Terminator X

From a rebel it's final on black vinyl
Soul, rock and roll comin' like a rhino
Tables turn – suckers burn to learn
They can't dis-able the power of my label
Def Jam – tells you who I am
The enemy's public – they really give a damn
Strong Island – where I got 'em wild and
That's the reason they're claimin' that I'm violent
Never silent – no dope gettin' dumb nope
Claimin' where we get our rhythm from
Number one – we hit ya and we give ya some
No gun – and still never on the run
You wanna be an S.1 – Griff will tell you when
And then you'll come – you'll know what time it is
Impeach the president – pullin' out the ray-gun
Zap the next one – I could be you're Sho-gun
Suckers – don't last a minute
Soft and smooth – I ain't with it
Hardcore – rawbone like a razor
I'm like a lazer – I just won't graze ya
Old enough to raise ya – so this will faze ya
Get it right boy and maybe I will praise ya
Playin' the role I got soul too
Voice my opinion with volume
Smooth – no what I am
Rough – cause I'm a man

No matter what the name – we're all the same
Pieces in one big chess game
Yeah – the voice of power
Is in the house – go take a shower boy
P.E. a group, a crew – not singular
We were black Wranglers
We're rap stranglers
You can't angle us – I know you're listenin'
I caught you pissin' in your pants You're scared of dissin' us
The crowd is missin' us
We're on a mission boy

Terminator X

Attitude – when I'm on fire
Juice on the loose – electric wire
Simple and plain – give me the lane
I'll throw it down your throat like Barkley
See the car keys – you'll never get these
They belong to the 98 Posse
You want some more son – you wanna get some
Rush the door of a store-pick up the album
You know the rhythm, the rhyme plus the beat is designed
So I can enter your mind – Boys
Bring the noise – my time
Step aside for the flex – Terminator X

PROPHETS OF RAGE

By Carlton Ridenhour, Eric Sadler & Hank Shocklee

© Copyright 1988. Lyrics reproduced by permission of Island Music Limited.
All Rights Reserved. International Copyright Secured.

With vice I hold the mike device
With force I keep it away of course
And I'm keepin' you from sleepin'
And on the stage I rage
And I'm rollin
To the poor I pour in on in metaphors
Not bluffin', it's nothin'
That we ain't did before
We played you stayed
The points made
You consider it done
By the prophets of rage
(Power of the people say)

I roll with the punches so I survive
Try to rock 'cause it keeps the crowd alive
I'm not ballin, I'm just callin'
But I'm past the days of yes y'allin
Wa wiggle round and round
I pump, you jump up
Hear my words my verbs
And get juiced up
I been around a while
You can describe my sound
Clear the way
For the prophets of rage
(Power of the people say)

I rang ya bell
Can you tell I got feelin'
Just peace at least
Cause I want it
Want it so bad
That I'm starvin'
I'm like Garvey
So you can see B
It's like that, I'm like Nat
Leave me the hell alone
If you don't think I'm a brother
Then check the chromosomes
Then check the stage
I declare it a new age
Get down for the prophets of rage
Keep you from gettin' like this

You back the track
You find we're the quotable
You emulate
Brothers, sisters, that's beautiful
Follow a path
Of positivity you go
Some sing it or rap it
Or harmonize it through Go-Go
Little you know but very
Seldom I do party jams
About a plan

I'm considered the man
I'm the recordable
But God made it affordable
I say it, you play it
Back in your car or even portable
Stereo
Describes my scenario
Left or right, Black or White
They tell lies in the books
That you're readin'
It's knowledge of yourself
That you're needin'
Like Vescey or Prosser
We have a reason why
To debate the hate
That's why we're born to die
Mandela, cell dweller, Thatcher
You can tell her clear the way for the prophets of rage
(Power of the people say)

It's raw and keepin' you on the floor
Its soul and keepin' you in control
It's pt. 2 cause I'm
Pumpin' what you're used to
Until the whole juice crew
Gets me in my goose down
I do the rebel yell
And I'm the duracell
Call it plain insane
Brothers causin' me pain
When a brother's a victim
And the sellers a dweller in a cage
Yo, run the accapella
(Power of the people say)

PARTY FOR YOUR RIGHT TO FIGHT

By Carlton Ridenhour, Eric Sadler & Hank Shocklee

Power Equality
And we're out to get it
I know some of you ain't wit'it
This party started right in '66
With a pro-Black radical mix
Then at the hour of twelve
Some force cut the power
And emerged from hell
It was your so called government
That made this occur
Like the grafted devils they were

J. Edgar Hoover, and he coulda' proved to 'ya
He had King and X set up
Also the party with Newton, Cleaver
  and Seale
He ended – so get up
Time to get 'em back-You got it
Get back on the track – You got it
Word from the honorable Elijah Muhammed
Know who you are to be Black

To those that disagree, it causes static
For the original Black Asiatic man
Cream of the earth
And was here first
And some devils prevent this from being known
But you check out the books they own
Even masons they know it
But refuse to show it – Yo
But it's proven and fact
And it takes a nation of millions
  to hold us back

© Copyright 1988. Lyrics reproduced by permission of Island Music Limited. All Rights Reserved. International Copyright Secured.